SUMMER

OF FIRE

SUMMER OF FIRE

YELLOWSTONE 1988

By Patricia Lauber

ORCHARD BOOKS   NEW YORK

FOR BECKY CHAMBERS,
the best friend a writer could hope for,
with long-standing appreciation and affection

ACKNOWLEDGMENTS
The author would like to thank the many people at
Yellowstone National Park who helped her with the research
and making of this book by giving generously of their time
and expertise, most particularly Gillian Bowser, entomologist;
Don G. Despain, research biologist; Ronald Jones, Fisheries,
U.S. Fish and Wildlife Service; Jim Peaco, photo specialist;
Roy Renkin, naturalist; George Robinson, chief,
Interpretation; Sandra Robinson, Public Affairs.

Frontispiece: Most of Yellowstone's forests are lodgepole pine,
here seen in a view from the forest floor.

Orchard Books
A division of Franklin Watts, Inc.
387 Park Avenue South
New York, NY 10016

Manufactured in Hong Kong
Printed and bound by Toppan Printing Company, Inc.
Book design by Kathleen Westray
Typesetting by A & S Graphics, Inc.

10 9 8 7 6 5 4 3 2 1

The text of this book is set in 12 point Galliard.
The illustrations are full-color photographs.

Library of Congress Cataloging-in-Publication Data
Lauber, Patricia.
Summer of fire : Yellowstone 1988 / by Patricia Lauber.
p.   cm.   Includes bibliographical references and index.
Summary: Describes the season of fire that struck Yellowstone
in 1988, and examines the complex ecology that returns plant
and animal life to a seemingly barren, ash-covered expanse.
ISBN 0-531-05943-X. — ISBN 0-531-08543-0 (lib.)
1. Forest fires—Yellowstone National Park—Juvenile literature.
2. Forest ecology—Yellowstone National Park—Juvenile literature.
3. Yellowstone National Park—Juvenile literature.   [1. Forest
fires—Yellowstone National Park.   2. Fire ecology.   3. Ecology.
4. Yellowstone National Park.   5. National parks and reserves.]   I. Title.
SD421.32.Y45L38   1991
581.5′2642—dc20   90-23032

CONTENTS

YELLOWSTONE

YELLOWSTONE National Park lies in the Rocky Mountains, filling the northwestern corner of Wyoming and spilling over into Idaho and Montana. The heart of the park is a high plateau, born of gigantic volcanic eruptions. The last of these took place some 600,000 years ago. It was so great that volcanic ash fell on large parts of North America. Dust, carried on the winds, circled the earth and dimmed the sun's light.

The cause of the eruption was a huge pocket of hot rock inside the earth, rock so hot that it was molten. The name for such rock is magma. Over hundreds of thousands of years, magma filled the pocket and pushed upward. The ground above swelled, bulged, stretched, and cracked open. Hot gases, ash, and chunks of solid rock exploded out of the earth. Later, smaller eruptions poured out floods of lava that covered the land.

Castle Geyser erupts, and its spray breaks up the sun's white light, forming a rainbow.

Magma heats rock of the earth's crust under Yellowstone National Park. The rock heats water that has seeped down from the surface, raising its temperature above the boiling point. But the water does not boil, because it is under great pressure. It circulates through cracks and other openings in the rock and in time finds its way to the surface. Depending on its temperature and the kind of opening that leads to the surface, the water may burst out of the earth as a geyser, turn to steam, or bubble up as a hot spring. The hot water and steam bring minerals to the surface. They often form strange shapes. Castle Geyser was named by early explorers because its shape reminded them of a crumbling turret on a castle.

West Thumb on Yellowstone Lake has hot springs, pools, steam vents *(left)*, and lakeside geysers *(above)*.

The roar of steam and gases rushing toward the surface earned this hill its name: Roaring Mountain.

A pocket of magma still lies beneath the plateau, and someday another great eruption will take place. But at present the magma accounts for the sights that make Yellowstone famous. It heats groundwater that shoots out of the earth as geysers, bubbles up as hot springs, steams out of vents, and churns mud pots. Other parks in the United States also have lofty mountains, forests and meadows, and many kinds of wildlife. But only Yellowstone has thousands of geysers, hot springs, and steam vents. Only Yellowstone has strange and eerie landscapes formed of minerals carried to the surface by hot water. Every year some two and a half million people are drawn to the sights of Yellowstone. They come from all over the world to see the park.

Visitors who arrived in the summer of 1988 saw something else, something that no one had seen in more than 200 years—forest fires so big that thousands of fire fighters could not put them out. The red and yellow flames marked both the end of an old story in Yellowstone and the beginning of a new one.

The terraces at Mammoth are built of minerals carried to the surface by hot springs and steam. From time to time the courses taken by hot water and steam change, and new terraces are built.

The colors seen at hot springs, such as Morning Glory Pool, are those of tiny plants, called blue-green algae, and of bacteria. The algae can live in water as hot as 167 degrees Fahrenheit, and bacteria can live in even hotter water.

SUMMER
OF FIRE

THE summer of 1988 was hot and dry in much of the United States. Above plains and prairies, the sun blazed out of an ever blue sky, baking fields and withering crops. Ponds and streams dried up. Rivers shrank. In places the very earth cracked open as underground water supplies dwindled away.

Farther west, forests were tinder dry. Sometimes skies grew dark with storm clouds. Thunder growled and lightning crackled, but little rain fell. Lightning strikes started forest fires that raged across the Rockies and other ranges with the roar of jumbo jets on take-off. Night skies turned red and yellow where flames soared 300 feet into the air. Smoke, carried on the winds, darkened skies as far away as Spokane and Minneapolis–St. Paul. Airline passengers, flying high above the fires, could smell the smoke. Before the rains and snows of autumn came, 2,600,000 acres had burned in the West and Alaska, an area twice the size of Delaware.

In the summer drought of 1988 lightning strikes started wildfires across the northern Rockies.

YELLOWSTONE FIRES
August 16, 1988, 8:00 a.m.

North Entrance

Mammoth Hot Springs

Tower-Roosevelt

Northeast Entrance

Fan Fire

Clover-Mist Fire

Norris

Canyon

Madison Fire

Madison

West Entrance

Lovely Fire

Fishing Bridge

Lake

Bridge Bay

East Entrance

Old Faithful

West Thumb

Cub Fire

North Fork Fire

Shoshone Lake

Grant Village

Yellowstone Lake

Lewis Lake

Continental-Ridge Fire

Falls Fire

Red-Shoshone Fire

Heart Lake

Mink Creek Fire

South Entrance

In Yellowstone the fire season started on May 24, when lightning struck a tree in the northeastern part of the park. The fire stayed small. Rain fell later in the day and put it out. That was what usually happened. In Yellowstone, winters are long and cold, summers short and often rainy. Many people thought you couldn't set fire to the forest if you tried.

On June 23 lightning started a fire near Shoshone Lake in the southern part of the park. On June 25 another bolt of lightning started a fire in the northwest. These fires did not go out, and no one tried to put them out. Park policy was to let wildfires burn unless they threatened lives or property. Also, there seemed no reason to worry about the fires. Although winters in the 1980s had been dry, with little snow, summers had been unusually wet. The summer of 1988 was expected to be wet too.

But in 1988 the rains of summer did not come. The Shoshone and other fires blazed and spread. By mid-July, 8,600 acres had burned. Park officials decided that all fires should be put out, no matter whether they were wildfires or caused by human carelessness.

Flames raced through forests when rain failed to come.

Fire fighters arrived by the hundreds to attack fires from the ground. Helicopters and airplanes attacked from above. But new fires started in the park. In 1988 Yellowstone had more than 50 lightning strikes, twice the normal number. Fires in neighboring national forests swept into the park. Old fires burned on. And still the rains did not come.

Cold fronts passed through, bringing winds of hurricane force with gusts of 60 to 80 miles an hour. Winds whipped and spread the fires and fed them oxygen, which fires must have to keep burning. Big fires met, merged, and became even bigger fires. In forests flames galloped through the tops, or crowns, of trees, through the canopy. Snags—dead trees that

Fire fighters could put out small blazes . . .

but they were helpless in the face of big ones.

are still standing—burned like Roman candles. Boulders exploded in the heat. Sheets of flame leaped forward. Gigantic clouds of smoke ringed the horizon, looking like thunderheads, only bigger. There were days when the sun was no brighter than a full moon.

Fires jumped rivers, roads, canyons, parking lots. Glowing embers, some the size of a man's fist, shot a mile or more ahead, starting new fires. Flames were roaring through the park at a rate of four or five miles a day. One fire ran 14 miles in only four hours. On August 20, a day known as Black Saturday, more than 150,000 acres burned inside the park and in neighboring forests. The 2,000 fire fighters could no more put out these fires than they could have stopped a hurricane. But what they could do was defend the park communities—the information centers and the buildings where people slept, ate, and shopped.

By September 6 fire fighters were moving in to defend the area around the park's most famous geyser, Old Faithful. The geyser itself could not be harmed by fire, but the buildings around it could. One of them, the Old Faithful Inn, was the world's largest log building. Now one of the eight major fires in the park was bearing down on it.

Cold air and smoke were trapped in mountain valleys by an upper layer of warm air.

Long hours of hard work tired the women and men who fought the fires.

Clouds of smoke looked like thunderheads, only bigger.

Flames rocketed into the crowns of trees.

Called the North Fork fire, it had started in the Targhee National Forest on July 22, when a careless woodcutter threw away a lighted cigarette. Driven by shifting winds, the fire raced into Yellowstone, turned back into Targhee, neared the town of West Yellowstone, then veered back into the park. There it jumped roads and rivers, snarling its way through the crossroads at Madison on August 15. By the afternoon of September 7 it was approaching Old Faithful. Long before they could see the flames, fire fighters heard the fire's deep rumble and saw a churning wall of dark smoke towering skyward.

Planes dropped chemicals to damp down fires. On the ground weary fire fighters were wetting down buildings.

The fire came on, a mass of red flames whipped by winds gusting up to 50 miles an hour. Sparks and embers were everywhere, flying over the inn, parking lots, and geyser, and setting fire to the woods beyond. At the last moment the wind shifted and the fire turned to the northeast, away from Old Faithful.

Saturday, September 10, began as another bad day. One arm of the North Fork fire was threatening park headquarters at Mammoth Hot Springs, and another arm was a quarter of a mile from Tower Junction. The forecast was for winds of up to 60 miles an hour. But the sky was thick with clouds, and the temperature was falling.

By early afternoon, September 10 had turned into a day of hope. Rain was drenching the area around Old Faithful. The next morning snow blew along the streets of West Yellowstone. It sifted through blackened forests and dusted herds of bison and elk. Scattered islands of fire would burn until November blanketed them in snow. But the worst was over.

At long last the summer of fire had ended. During

it, eight major fires and many smaller ones had burned in Yellowstone. To people who had watched the fires on television news, it seemed the park must lie in ruins. But this was not so. The geysers, steam vents, and hot springs were unharmed. Park communities had been saved. Nearly two-thirds of the park had not even been touched by fire.

It was true that many once-green areas were now black and gray. Yet it was also true that they were not ruined. Instead, they were beginning again, starting over, as they had many times in the past. Fire has always been part of the Yellowstone region. Wildfire has shaped the landscape and renewed it. Yellowstone needs fire, just as it needs sun and rain, and its plants have developed ways of surviving fire.

Pockets of flames and embers continued to burn after the worst was over.

Finally the snows of November put an end to the fires.

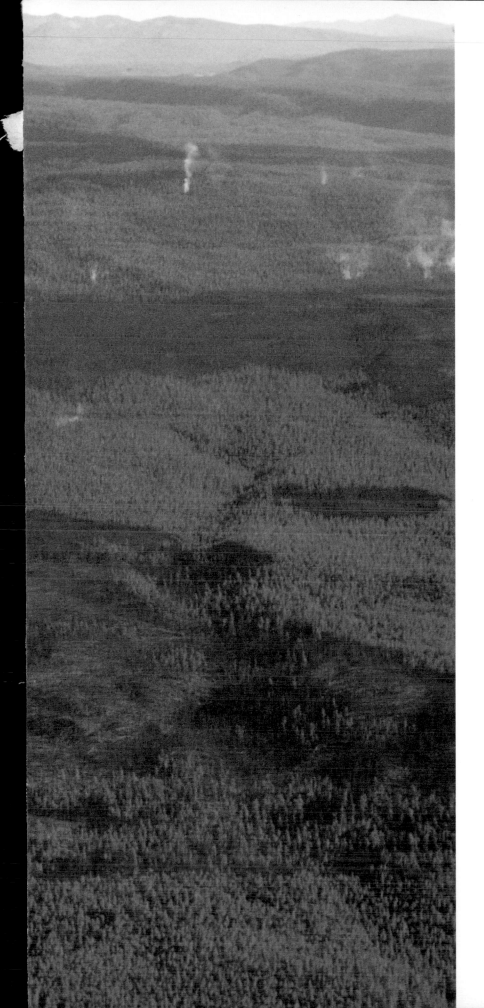

THE FORESTS
AND THE FIRES

WHEN the air cleared in late September, park scientists were able to fly over Yellowstone. They found that fires had raged in about one third of it, but just some of that third had burned. Less than 1 percent of the park had been turned to ashes.

Fire does not advance as a solid wall of flames, destroying everything in its path. It hops and jumps, often over large areas. It sends out arms and tendrils, twisting this way and that. Seen from the air, parts of the park had large black areas with islands of green. It had large green areas with islands of black. It was a patchwork quilt of black and green, of heavy burns and light burns.

Fires created a patchwork quilt of green and black areas.

A meadow that looked dead in November of 1988 . . .

Flames had swept quickly through meadows. They burned dead matter. They burned off the tops of plants but did not harm the roots. Some places that burned in July were green again in September, as roots sent up new sprouts. By the following summer there was only one way to tell which meadows had burned. They were richer and greener than meadows that had not burned. They were greener because fire had fertilized them.

was green and lush in July of 1989.

To live and grow, plants need nourishment, or nutrients, which they take from the soil. The nutrients are minerals that dissolve in water and are taken up by a plant's roots. That is, they become locked up in the plant. For soil to stay fertile, the mineral nutrients must somehow be replaced in it. Farmers and gardeners may fertilize soil by adding nutrients to it. In nature the same mineral nutrients are used over and over again—they are recycled.

Where forests had burned, meadows sprang up.

Although nutrients are locked up in plants, plant parts keep dying. Flowers, leaves, twigs, and branches fall to the ground, carrying nutrients with them. Whole plants die and fall. Still more nutrients are locked up in animals that eat plants. Some fall to the ground in animal droppings, some when animals die. But before other plants can use these nutrients, they must be released from dead matter— somehow the dead matter must be broken down.

In regions that are warmer and wetter than Yellowstone, this job is done by earthworms, beetles, millipedes, fungi, bacteria, and other small forms of life. They feed on dead matter and break it down— they cause it to rot away, or decay. Minerals are then returned to the soil. In a region like Yellowstone, decay takes place very slowly, because the small forms of life are active only during the short warm season. Dead branches take years to rot away. A tree trunk may take a hundred years. Here fire is needed to return minerals to the soil. It releases them quickly from dead matter in a form that plants can use. It releases them in meadows and in forests. It has been doing this for as long as there have been forests in the northern Rockies.

Most of Yellowstone's forests are lodgepole pine. Lodgepoles are tall, slender trees, so named because Indians used them to make lodges and tepees.

In a forest of young lodgepoles, grasses and flowering plants cover the forest floor. The trees grow slowly in the cold climate of Yellowstone. Fifty years may pass before they are 30 to 50 feet tall. By then they form thick stands of 200 to 300 trees to an acre and they are competing for light, water, and nutrients. Their crowns grow together, forming a canopy that shuts off light from the forest floor. Grasses and flowers can no longer grow there.

Lodgepoles are tall, slender trees that drop their lower branches as they grow.

As lodgepoles compete and age, some die. Because the trees have shallow roots, they are easily toppled by strong winds. Trunks, branches, twigs, cones, and needles litter the forest floor and do not rot away. In an aging lodgepole forest, trees may lack space and minerals. They weaken and are likely to be attacked by disease or insects such as the mountain pine beetle.

Thousands of these tiny beetles bore into a tree, where they lay their eggs. They also carry a fungus. The fungus attacks the sapwood, the layer of the tree that carries water and nutrients from the roots to the crown. When the eggs hatch, the beetle young attack the cambium, the tree layer that makes new wood. They attack the inner bark, the layer of the tree that carries food to the cambium and roots. The aging tree dies. In only three years mountain pine beetles may kill an entire stand of lodgepoles. If lightning strikes these trees, they burn like so much kindling wood.

In 1984 a tornado-like wind swept through Yellowstone, felling a large number of lodgepoles, which have shallow roots. The fallen trees burned during the fires of 1988.

In old lodgepole forests, Engelmann spruce and subalpine fir take hold.

Fires are rare in young lodgepole forests. The trees are widely spaced. The forest floor is carpeted with moist green plants. Fire cannot spread readily.

Fires are also rare among lodgepoles that are 50 to 100 years old, because there is little fuel for fire. Fire may crawl along the ground, burning needles, cones, and branches. But it cannot climb into the canopy, because lodgepoles are self-pruning trees— as they grow, their lower branches drop off. There is no ladder of branches that fire can climb.

As a forest grows older, though, its floor becomes a seedbed for two other kinds of trees: Engelmann spruce and subalpine fir. When these trees are young, they grow well in shade. If fire comes to such a forest, it burns the spruce and firs, which are not self-pruning. It climbs them and rockets into the crowns of the lodgepoles. The canopy bursts into flames. Dead trees add fuel. Hot air rises, and oxygen-rich air is sucked in from all around. The roaring blaze becomes a tornado of fire.

If fire comes, spruce and fir serve as a ladder that fire climbs into the forest canopy.

When the fire moves on, it leaves behind blackened skeletons of trees. Gray-black ash hides the ground. Here and there tree ghosts can be seen—marks left on the ground by fallen trees that burned like logs in a fireplace. It is hard to believe that any kind of life has survived here. Yet there are many ways in which plants of the northern Rockies do survive fire. In nature survival does not have to mean that a plant is still alive. It usually means that the plant has left a way of producing new plants, that the kind of plant will continue.

Many of the plants in Yellowstone have developed ways of surviving fire. That is, they are adapted to fire. The lodgepole pine is one of these.

The seeds of lodgepoles form inside cones. There are two kinds of cones. One kind simply opens and frees its seeds. The seeds are winged and they whirl away from the parent plant. That is how lodgepoles usually reproduce. The second kind of cone is sealed tight by a thick coat of resin and is hard as a rock. These cones open only in high heat—at least 113 degrees Fahrenheit. In the blackened forests scientists found 50,000 to 1,000,000 lodgepole seeds to an acre. All had come from sealed cones that were opened by the heat of fire. Most would become food for small animals, but some would sprout. The burned forest was a perfect place for them to grow. The soil was rich in nutrients, and there was plenty of sunlight. By the summer of 1989 each was an inch-high stem bearing some eight needles—a young tree, born of fire.

Douglas firs, which grow in the lower parts of Yellowstone, are also adapted to fire. Like the lodgepoles, they are self-pruning. No lower branches offer a ladder for fire to climb. Unlike lodgepoles the older trees have thick bark. It protects them from fire.

Sealed cones open only in high heat.

A sealed cone released its seeds on the burned forest floor. Two sprouted next to the cone—their seed coverings can still be seen in this photograph.

When autumn comes, aspen turn gold.

Some trees are adapted in another way. If they are injured in a fire, they produce bumper crops of seeds. They may live for only two or three years, but the kind of tree does not die out.

Most trees reproduce only from seeds, but a few kinds have a second way of making more of themselves. Their roots send up new shoots. Willow is one of these trees. Aspen is another.

Aspen are thin-barked trees that grow in groves. Under the grove is a huge root system that is shared by all the trees. When the trees are alive and healthy, the roots do not send up many shoots. A chemical in the leaves and buds keeps them from doing so. When fire sweeps a grove, the leaves and buds are killed. Now the root system sends up thousands of new shoots. They grow quickly because they do not have to form a root system to take water and nutrients from the soil. The roots are already in place.

One year after the fires, young plants were everywhere in the burned areas. There were leafy green shoots and tiny trees. Years earlier shrubs had grown among young lodgepoles. Then the pines shaded out the shrubs. Seeds dropped by the shrubs lay on the forest floors. Now those seeds sprang to life.

Because of the patchwork of green and black, no burned area was far from a source of other seeds. Small ones blew in on the wind. The seeds of fireweed and dandelion drifted in on silky parachutes. Seeds arrived with animals—in the coats of mammals, in the droppings of birds and mammals, and on the feet and feathers of birds. Flowers and other leafy plants grew from these seeds.

The return of plant life was important to the animals of Yellowstone. Many feed on plants, eating seeds, sprouts, blades of grass, and other plant parts. And these animals are in turn food for other animals. The park's plants and animals fit together in a big web of life.

Given sunlight, nutrients, and rain, larkspur bloomed on the burned forest floor.

THE ANIMALS
AND THE FIRES

DURING the fires of 1988, many people imagined animals fleeing in terror, with flames about to overtake them. But that was not what happened. Most animals simply moved out of the way as fires approached.

The nesting season was over, and birds flew off to places where there were no fires. Elk, deer, bison, moose, and other large mammals walked away from the fires. Often they fed or bedded down in a meadow while a forest crackled and burned nearby. Many small mammals were able to outrun the fires. Others were safe underground in their burrows, where the soil shielded them from heat. Only a small number of mammals were killed, mostly by smoke.

Like other big hoofed mammals, bison bedded down or fed while fires raged nearby.

For many animals, both inside and outside the park, the fires offered opportunity. Burned forests often buzzed with life before they had even cooled.

Wood-boring beetles arrived, perhaps attracted by the smoke. So did horn-tailed wasps, which scientists had not seen in the park before. Both came to lay their eggs in dead or dying trees. Their young fed on inner bark and cambium, carving holes and tunnels through the wood.

The arrival of insects attracted large numbers of woodpeckers. These birds drill into trees to feed on insects and their young. Woodpeckers also drill nest-

The Uinta ground squirrel sleeps away the hot months of July and August in its burrow. It was safely out of the way during the worst of the fires.

ing holes in trees. Once they have raised their young, they abandon the holes and make new ones the next year. The old holes are used by birds that nest in holes but cannot make their own—mountain bluebirds, tree swallows, black-capped chickadees. Woodpeckers usually move on to another burned area after two to five years. But their holes are used for a long time by the bluebirds, swallows, and chickadees. They live and raise their young in the burned forest and feed on insects and other bugs.

Bugs that lived aboveground either flew away or were killed in the fires. Other small creatures had

A three-toed woodpecker has drilled
a nest hole in a dead tree.

The mountain bluebird uses nest holes
abandoned by woodpeckers.

Fresh, green meadows made possible the return of aboveground insects.

Golden-mantled ground squirrels could hide in their burrows as fires roared through forests, but like other small mammals in burned areas, many were captured by meat-eating animals.

Coyotes are hunters of small mammals . . .

as are screech owls and other birds of prey.

nests underground or made their homes beneath rocks and logs. They survived. Even when the fires were still burning, scientists could turn over a rock or log and find millipedes, centipedes, wood beetles, mites, and colonies of small ants. On fire-warm forest floors, ants were busily gathering seeds and carrying these back to their nests. Many kinds of aboveground insects returned in 1989 as meadows came up fresh and green and flowers bloomed. The plants offered them food, as well as places for egg laying and hiding.

After the fires had passed through, the ground-dwelling bugs were food for many birds and for small mammals, such as shrews. Birds also arrived to feed on the lodgepole pine seeds. Small mammals gathered them. Chipmunks and squirrels scampered about, cheeks bulging with seeds. But the ground was bare. Only a few small islands of grass offered hiding places for shrews, mice, voles, chipmunks, and squirrels. And so these animals became easy meals for coyotes, foxes, and weasels, as well as owls, hawks, eagles, herons, and cranes.

From time to time elk and bison wandered through the burned forests looking for food.

Sometimes elk or bison wandered through the burned forests, feeding on stems and leaves sent up by the roots of grasses. Summer and fall were hard for them. Both drought and fire had cut back their food supply. Many elk turned to less nourishing sources of food, such as pine needles. They began an early move to their winter feeding grounds, where the land is lower and the climate is warmer. But some of these feeding grounds had also burned. Of the big hoofed mammals only the moose were able to find food easily. Much of the time they eat plants that grow in lakes and streams.

Moose find food in lakes and streams.

By mid-November winter had settled into Yellowstone. Bitter cold gripped the land, and heavy snows fell. Some elk found food beside the geysers and hot springs, where heat melted snow and bared the ground. In long files bison also trudged to these places. But the months of drought, fire, and now winter proved too much for the feeble, the old, and the very young.

Yet, other animals benefited as winter thinned the herds of elk and bison. Coyotes, foxes, weasels, and ravens feasted on the winter kills. So did black bears and grizzlies, when they woke from their winter's sleep and left their dens in spring.

The coming of spring brought a slow melting of the heavy snow pack. Water seeped through ash into the ground. It ran off into streams and rivers. In it were nutrients for plants of the land and for plants of the waters that are home to Yellowstone's trout.

Trout feed on water insects—mayflies, caddis flies, stone flies, and others. And the insects feed on plant matter. Some feed by scraping algae off rocks. Some feed by shredding plant matter that grows in or falls into the streams and rivers. When forests and meadows were burning, shredders lost much of their food supply. But with the coming of summer, there was more food than before the fires.

Bison made their way to places where the heat of geysers and hot springs had melted snow and bared the ground.

Meadows grew back along the banks of streams. Leafy plants sprang up on the floors of burned forests, adding to the food supply. Once streams had flowed through shady, cool forests. Where forests had burned, streams were now warmed by the sun. In the warmer, nutrient-rich waters, plant life flourished. It flourished in streams and also in lakes fed by the streams. With more food, insects flourished. So did the trout. And trout are an important food for the fish-eaters of the park—bears and otters, eagles, herons, osprey, pelicans, and others.

Nutrients from the ash fertilized meadows. Elk and bison grazed in them and browsed on the tender shoots that aspen were sending up. Small mammals again had hiding places. Hummingbirds sipped nectar from flowers and helped to pollinate them. Aboveground insects flew or blew in from other parts of the park.

Fireweed is one of the first plants to appear after a fire. Its pink flowers were everywhere. Hawkmoths laid their eggs on its leaves, which their caterpillar young would eat. Tiny green aphids sucked juices from the leaves. Ants guarded the aphids and milked them for their sugary honeydew.

Carpenter ants invaded burned forests and began hollowing out dead trees to make nesting sites. They became food for birds and small mammals. Wood-boring beetles went on carving tunnels in trees. Bees made their homes in beetle holes. Woodpeckers fed on beetle young. Mourning cloak butterflies sucked up sap that ran from woodpecker holes. On the ground, chipmunks were still gathering the seeds of lodgepole pines.

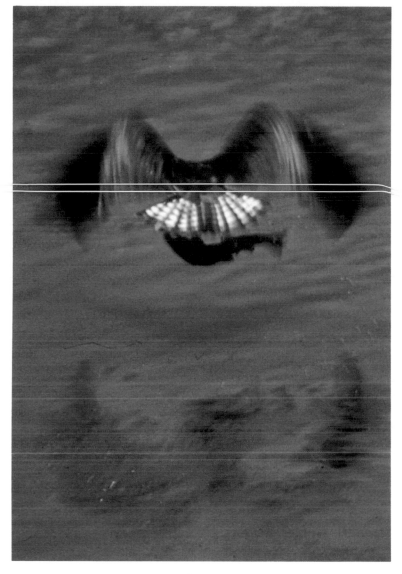

An osprey flies off with its catch, a trout.

By the summer of 1989 life of some kind was everywhere in the park. And so were natural scientists—watching, measuring, counting, studying, experimenting. All wanted the same thing: to learn more about the changes that keep the park a home for many kinds of plants and animals.

Fireweed, which appears soon after fires, became food for hawkmoth caterpillars and for aphids.

WEBS OF LIFE AND FIRES

SCIENTISTS knew that big fires had always been part of the Yellowstone region. But the last big fires took place 200 to 300 years ago. At that time there were no scientists around to observe what happened afterward. Today's scientists were eager to see how life comes back to burned areas. The fires of 1988 gave them a chance to learn more about how nature works.

Sometimes scientists learn just by being sharp-eyed. One found a tiny Douglas fir seedling in an area that had been heavily burned. He was surprised, because the cones and seeds of Douglas firs burn up in fires. Where had the seedling come from? He looked about and saw the answer: several cones were lying on the ground near the opening to a burrow. Before the fire a small mammal had stored away some cones. After the fire it had brought out cones to feed on the seeds. It lost a seed, and the seed sprouted. If all went well, the seedling would grow into a tree, with cones and seeds. Some seeds would become new trees, some food for small animals.

Big fires have always been part of the Yellowstone region.

About a fifth of the park's whitebark pines burned in 1988. The cones of this tree have big seeds that grizzly bears eat when they are fattening up for their winter's sleep. The seeds are also a favorite food of a bird called Clark's nutcracker. The nutcracker harvests seeds by picking them out of cones with its long, strong beak. Later it makes holes in the ground and stores its seeds. Sometimes the bird forgets where it has hidden some seeds. It does not come back to eat them, and the seeds sprout. Whitebark pines take root. Some scientists are asking, Do these seeds reach burned areas only with the help of Clark's nutcracker? Or are there other ways that the seeds spread? They are trying to find out.

Grizzlies eat many kinds of food, among them seeds of the whitebark pine.

Clark's nutcracker also eats the seeds of whitebark pine. The bird harvests seeds and stores them in soil, where they sometimes sprout and grow into new trees.

Bugs are important to the life of meadows and forests. They break up soil, letting air in. They play a part in rot. And they serve as food for many small animals.

If an area has been heavily burned, how quickly do bugs colonize it? One scientist designed an experiment to find out. She took a number of boards of the same size, which would serve as logs. She placed some in unburned areas and an equal number in burned areas. During the summer of 1989, she kept identifying and counting all the bugs that made their homes under the boards—mites, centipedes, millipedes, ants, small beetles. In early summer there were many more bug colonies under the boards in the unburned areas. By late summer the kinds and numbers of bugs were almost the same in burned and unburned areas.

Another scientist wanted to know how plants colonize burned areas. Before fires arrived, he marked out some small plots of ground, using metal frames that would not burn. He identified and counted all the plants growing in the plots. After the fires had passed through, he began a study that will go on for a number of years: Which plants survived the fire and came up again? What new plants are colonizing the plots? What happens to the colonizers—do they take hold or die out? Are any of them plants that are not native to Yellowstone? Do the kinds of plants in the plots change over the years? If so, how fast do changes take place?

The park's elk spend the winter in places where little snow falls and food is not buried under drifts.

Some scientists are studying streams. The fires brought quick benefits to streams—nutrients from ash, more sunlight, more leafy plants along the banks. How long will the benefits go on? Suppose a winter's snow pack melts quickly. Will soil from the burned forests be carried off into the streams? How will this affect plants, insects, fish, and fish-eaters?

Burned-over meadows come back quickly with plants that are rich in nutrients. Will grazing animals move from their usual feeding grounds to the new meadows? Will they change the routes they take to reach water, bedding grounds, calving areas? Will they change their routes to winter and summer ranges? Those are questions other scientists are working to answer.

Still others are studying how lodgepole pine forests take hold again after a fire. They are asking, Does it matter what the forest was like before the fire—whether its trees had more open or more sealed cones? Does it matter whether a burn was heavy or light? Are there more seedlings in places where the trees burned up or in places where trees are still standing but dead?

Scientists would also like to know, Do large burned patches grow back at the same rate as small burned patches? They think the answer is no. Small patches ought to recover faster. No part of them is far from a place where plants are growing. So seeds need travel only a short distance to fall on fertile ground. But to be sure, scientists will wait and watch and count. Perhaps large patches grow back from edge to center, with seeds traveling in yearly jumps. Only time will tell.

Pelicans feed on the fish of the park's lakes and rivers.

There are many questions about aspen, which seems to have its own rules for growing. The root system may keep sending up shoots year after year. Or it may send up shoots that grow into shrubs. Sometimes, but not always, the shrubs grow into trees. What causes aspen to do one thing and not another? Does fire play a part? The amount of browsing by elk? Climate changes? Is there more than one answer?

Does aspen ever grow from seed? For years the answer seemed to be no. To sprout and take root, aspen seeds need three things.

They need soil made only of minerals, bare soil where no litter is rotting. A chemical in litter keeps aspen seeds from sprouting.

They need moisture during the whole growing season. Aspen cannot live in dry soil.

And they need a place where no other plants are growing. An aspen seed is tiny. This means there is little food stored in it for a young plant to use. Aspen must put its roots down quickly. It must put out leaves quickly. Then the seedling can take water and nutrients from the soil and can use sunlight to make food in its leaves. An aspen cannot compete with other plants, because the tiny seedling does not get enough sunlight.

Bare mineral soil, no other plants, lots of moisture—these three things are not often found together. Some people thought that Yellowstone's groves of aspen must have formed some 10,000 years ago, at the end of the Ice Age. That was a time when glaciers were melting and the land was wet, bare, and without plants. Perhaps some groves of aspen did get their start then. Perhaps they all did. But the fires of 1988 have given scientists a chance to see if aspen can also take hold after big fires.

Burned forest floors were free of litter and bare of plants. Some were near streams and marshes. And there scientists found thousands of aspen seedlings. What will happen to them? The best guess is that they will grow but only for a while. Then the lodgepole pines will make a comeback and shade out the aspen. But even the best guess is not an answer. To learn the answer, scientists must watch what happens with the passing of time.

Still other aspen seedlings are growing in the northern part of the park, where there are no lodgepole pine forests. Will these seedlings survive? All anyone can do is to wait and see.

As scientists watch and wait, many feel they are seeing a story unfold. In a way they already know and have lived through the end of the story: aging forests, dead trees, huge fires. Now they are seeing how the story starts. They are seeing the beginning. It is a story that has unfolded many times in Yellowstone over the centuries, always with the same ending. It is a story of change, of new life taking the place of old life.

Groves of aspen are usually found at lower altitudes in the park, as are Douglas firs.

THE FIRES OF CHANGE

FO R many years park policy was to put out all fires, both wildfires and those caused by people. Fires were put out to keep the park from changing, to keep it as it was.

In the 1960s a group of scientists pointed out that it was impossible to keep the park from changing. A park is not a museum, full of once-living things. It is a place of life, and the natural world never stands still.

Take away wildfire, these scientists said, and Yellowstone will become a park of aging forests, weakened by a lack of nutrients and attacked by insects and disease. Fire is not an enemy to be fought. It is part of nature. And it is needed to tend forests and meadows, to put nutrients back in the soil. Over the years small fires and big fires have created a patchwork of plant life—new meadows, young forests, middle-aged forests, and old forests. And the many kinds and ages of plants make possible many kinds of animal life. Lodgepole forests that burned 25 years ago have three times as many kinds of animals and plants as old forests do.

A Douglas fir becomes a flaming torch in the North Fork fire.

In 1972 park policy changed. Fires caused by people were to be put out. But wildfires were to burn without being fought as long as they did not threaten human lives or property. For years everyone thought the policy worked well. Fires started and burned. Rain put them out. Then came a time of drought, with little snow in winter and little rain in summer. The year was 1988, the summer of fire. Now voices were raised in anger, saying park policy was wrong. All fires should have been fought. Because they weren't, the park was ruined.

To visit the blackened forests is to understand why people were upset. But the truth is that the park still has everything it had before the fires. Most of what burned was old lodgepole pine, trees that started to grow in the early 1700s, after an earlier great fire. It is also true that some of the biggest fires were fought from the very beginning and that human beings could not put them out. The end came only when the seasons changed and rain and snow damped the fires of summer.

Today geysers still shoot out of the ground, while hot springs bubble and steam. Snow-capped mountains tower above the park. In early summer bison and elk graze on new grasses. The bears are feasting on greenery. In the branchless forests of dead trees, the blackened floors soak up the sun's heat, and new life is triggered.

A mule deer fawn awaits the return of its mother.

A red fox returns from hunting to her burrow and young.

Spring and early summer are a time of renewal, of new life. Plants are freshly green, wildflowers bloom, and everywhere young animals start to learn about the world around them.

Tired of playing, young bison rest while their parents feed.

A bobcat kitten is ready to play or feed.

A black bear cub looks around.

Skeleton trees are losing their charred bark. In time the trees will weather to a silvery gray. A meadow of flowers and grasses will grow around them.

As the years pass, a new lodgepole pine forest will form. The lodgepoles will start to thin themselves out. Dead trees will fall. In another 200 years the meadow will be gone. In its place will be a forest of tall lodgepoles, their crowns growing together in a canopy. Young spruce and firs will grow on the shady forest floor, but not much else will live in the forests.

And then will come a time of drought, heat, high winds, and storm clouds that bring lightning but little rain. Once more the story will end as wildfires blaze in old forests. Once more it will begin again as the first green shoots push up through the gray and black of forest floors.

Once charred bark peels from trees, they will start to weather and turn silvery gray.

GLOSSARY

Definitions refer to the way terms are used in this book.

aphid A small insect that feeds by sucking sap from plants. It gives off a sweet, sticky liquid called honeydew.

ash Tiny bits of molten rock that have cooled and hardened.

bacteria Certain one-celled forms of life that can be seen only with a microscope.

bug A general name for insects and other creatures with hard outside coverings and no bones.

burrow A hole or tunnel dug by a small animal as a place to live or hide.

cambium The layer of a tree that produces new sapwood and new bark. The new wood causes the tree to grow in diameter.

canopy The high covering of a forest, where crowns of trees grow together.

centipede A wormlike bug with many pairs of legs.

climate Average weather over a long period of time.

cold front *See* front.

colonize To establish a group of new settlers, which can be plants or animals.

crown The top of a tree.

front The boundary zone between two large masses of air that have different temperatures. When a mass of cold, dry air is moving faster than a mass of warmer air, it pushes under the warm air and forms a cold front. Stormy weather with high winds is likely to follow.

fungus (plural: **fungi**) A very simple plant that lacks the green coloring matter called chlorophyll and cannot make its own food. It takes its nourishment from other living things or from once-living things, such as dead trees.

geyser A natural hot spring that from time to time throws a column of water and steam into the air.

ice age A time when large parts of the land are covered with sheets of ice a mile or more thick. The last ice age, which is called the Ice Age, ended about 10,000 years ago.

insect A bug with six legs.

lava Molten rock from inside the earth that has reached the surface.

magma Molten rock inside the earth.

millipede A wormlike bug with legs attached in double pairs.

mite A bug that is related to spiders and ticks.

molten Melted by heat.

mud pot Mud that bubbles because steam is rising through it.

nutrient Something that nourishes. Plants take nutrients out of the soil in the form of minerals.

oxygen One of the gases in the earth's atmosphere. Fires cannot burn without oxygen.

plateau A high, fairly flat piece of land; a tableland.

policy A plan or course of action decided on ahead of time.

resin A kind of sticky sap that hardens.

sapwood The layer of a tree through which water and nutrients move from the roots to the crown.

snag A dead tree that is still standing.

steam vent A hole from which hot gases rush into the air. As they cool, they are seen as clouds of steam.

survival In nature survival usually means that the kind of plant or animal will go on existing.

thunderhead The swollen upper part of a thundercloud.

web of life A term used to describe the many links among plants and animals and their living places.

wildfire Fire with a natural cause, such as lightning.

FURTHER READING

* indicates a young people's book.

Conniff, Richard. "Yellowstone's 'rebirth' amid the ashes is not neat or simple, but it's real." *Smithsonian,* September 1989.

Hackett, Thomas. "Fire." *The New Yorker,* October 2, 1989.

Jeffrey, David. "Yellowstone: The Fires of 1988." *National Geographic,* February 1989.

Matthiessen, Peter. "The Case for Burning." *The New York Times Magazine,* December 11, 1988.

*Patent, Dorothy Hinshaw. *Yellowstone Fires: Flames and Rebirth.* New York: Holiday House, 1990.

Romme, William H., and Don G. Despain. "The Yellowstone Fires." *Scientific American,* November 1989.

Shively, Carol. "A Smoke-Scented Diary." *Natural History,* August 1989.

*Vogel, Carole Garbuny, and Kathryn Allen Goldner. *The Great Yellowstone Fire.* Boston: Sierra Club/Little Brown, 1990.

Williams, Ted. "The Incineration of Yellowstone." *Audubon,* January 1989.

Wuerthner, George. *Yellowstone and the Fires of Change.* Salt Lake City: Dream Garden Press, 1988.

INDEX

Illustrations and captions are indexed in *italics*.

ILLUSTRATION
CREDITS